SHORT WALKS LAKE DISTRICT

KESWICK, BORROWDALE
AND BUTTERMERE

by Vivienne Crow

Buttermere is surrounded by spectacular mountain scenery (Walk 2)

CONTENTS

USING THIS GUIDE

Routes in this book

In this book you will find a selection of easy or moderate walks suitable for almost everyone, including casual walkers and families with children, or for when you only have a short time to fill. The routes have been carefully chosen to allow you to explore the area and its attractions. Most routes are circular, although some linear walks may be included that use public transport to get back to the start. Although there may be some climbs there is no challenging terrain, but do bear in mind that conditions can sometimes be wet or muddy underfoot. A route summary table is included on page 6 to help you choose the right walk.

Clothing and footwear

You won't need any special equipment to enjoy these walks. The weather in Britain can be changeable, so choose clothing suitable for the season and wear or carry a waterproof jacket. For footwear, comfortable walking boots or trainers with a good grip are best. A small rucksack for drinks, snacks and spare clothing is useful. See www.adventuresmart.uk.

Walk descriptions

At the beginning of each walk you'll find all the information you need:

- start/finish location, with postcode and a what3words address to help you find it
- parking and transport information, estimated walking time, total distance and climb
- details of public toilets available along the route and where you can get refreshments
- a summary of the key highlights of the walk and what you might see

Timings given are the time to complete the walk at a reasonable walking pace. Allow extra time for extended stops or if walking with children.

The route is described in clear, easy-to-follow directions, with each waypoint marked on an accompanying map extract. It's a good idea to read the whole of the route instructions before setting out, so that you know what to expect.

Maps, GPX files and what3words

Extracts from the OS® 1:25,000 map accompany each route. GPX files for all the walks in this book are available to download at www.cicerone.co.uk/1202/gpx.

What3words is a free smartphone app which identifies every 3m square of the globe with a unique three-word address, e.g. ///destiny.cafe.sonic. For more information see https://what3words.com/products/what3words-app.

Walking with children

Even young children can be surprisingly strong walkers, but every family is different and you may need to adapt the timings given in this book to take that into account. Make sure you go at the pace of the slowest member and choose a walk with an exciting objective in mind, such as a cave, river, waterfall or picnic spot. Many of the walks can be shortened to suit – suggestions are included at the end of the route description.

Dogs

Sheep or cattle may be found grazing on a number of these walks. Keep dogs under control at all times so that they don't scare or disturb livestock or wildlife. Cattle, particularly cows with calves, may very occasionally pose a risk to walkers with dogs. If you ever feel threatened by cattle, you should let go of your dog's lead and let it run free.

Enjoying the countryside responsibly

Enjoy the countryside and treat it with respect to protect our natural environments. Stick to footpaths and take your litter home with you. When driving, slow down on rural roads and park considerately, or better still use public transport. For more details check out www.gov.uk/countryside-code.

The Countryside Code

Respect everyone

- be considerate to those living in, working in and enjoying the countryside
- leave gates and property as you find them
- do not block access to gateways or driveways when parking
- be nice, say hello, share the space
- follow local signs and keep to marked paths unless wider access is available

Protect the environment

- take your litter home – leave no trace of your visit
- do not light fires and only have BBQs where signs say you can
- always keep dogs under control and in sight
- dog poo – bag it and bin it – any public waste bin will do
- care for nature – do not cause damage or disturbance

Enjoy the outdoors

- check your route and local conditions
- plan your adventure – know what to expect and what you can do
- enjoy your visit, have fun, make a memory

ROUTE SUMMARY TABLE

WALK NAME	START POINT	TIME	DISTANCE
1. Rannerdale Knotts	Buttermere village	3hr	8km (5 miles)
2. Buttermere circuit	Buttermere village	2¼hr	7km (4¼ miles)
3. Borrowdale, Seathwaite and Seatoller	Seatoller	1¾hr	5.5km (3½ miles)
4. Rosthwaite and Stonethwaite	Rosthwaite	1¼hr	4.5km (2¾ miles)
5. Castle Crag	Rosthwaite	2¼hr	7km (4¼ miles)
6. Watendlath and Ashness Bridge	Rosthwaite	2½hr	7.5km (4¾ miles)
7. Derwentwater shore	Grange	2½hr	9.5km (6 miles)
8. Cat Bells	By boat from Keswick	2¾hr	6.5km (4 miles)
9. Friar's Crag and Castlehead	Keswick	2¼hr	7km (4¼ miles)
10. Castlerigg Stone Circle	Keswick	2¼hr	7.5km (4¾ miles)
11. Latrigg and Keswick Railway Path	Keswick	3hr	9.5km (6 miles)
12. Barrow	Braithwaite	2¼hr	5km (3¼ miles)
13. Seat How and the Whinlatter forests	Whinlatter Visitor Centre	2¼hr	6km (3¾ miles)
14. Dodd	Dodd Wood car park	2¼hr	5.5km (3½ miles)
15. Skiddaw	Gale Road parking area	4½hr	10km (6¼ miles)

HIGHLIGHTS

Low fell with lake and mountain views

Lake surrounded by mountains

Woods, river and farming hamlets

Traditional villages and attractive side valley

Woodland, rewarding climb to top of low fell

Isolated hamlet, oak woods and iconic views

Lake and woodland

Rocky ascent of low fell with magnificent views

Lakeshore, ancient woods and viewpoint

Ancient monument in atmospheric location

Low fell with good views, disused railway

Ridge walking on a low fell

Forest viewpoint

Forest, wildlife and a viewpoint

Summit of England's fourth highest mountain

SYMBOLS USED ON ROUTE MAPS

(S)   Start point

(F)   Finish point

(SF)   Start and finish at the same place

[4]➔   Waypoint

~   Route line

MAPPING IS SHOWN AT A SCALE OF 1:25,000

0 KM   0.25   0.5

0 miles   0.25

DOWNLOAD THE GPX FILES FOR FREE AT
www.cicerone.co.uk/1202/GPX

Evening stroll in Borrowdale (Walk 3)

INTRODUCTION

Buttermere reflection (Walk 2)

There are good reasons why the Lake District is regarded as one of the UK's top destinations for walking. There's the natural scenery – a wonderful combination of hills (known locally as fells) and valleys, with the occasional lake thrown in for good measure, all liberally sprinkled with areas of woodland. Then there's the cultural landscape – an environment that has been shaped by farming, by mineral extraction and by millennia of settlement.

Its compact nature, with roads criss-crossing the area, and relatively low fells, make the Lake District easily accessible compared with, say, the Scottish Highlands. Throw in an intricate network of paths and trails, as well as vast areas of access land, and you've got a region that is just crying out to be explored on foot.

Popular with tourists, it also benefits from a good range of facilities – plentiful accommodation, places to eat, and bus and boat services, for example – making it an 'easy' destination for visitors.

What to expect

Keswick, Borrowdale and Buttermere are situated in the north-western part of the Lake District National Park.

Keswick, the most populous town in the area, lies at the northern tip of Derwentwater, the third largest of the lakes. Heading south from Keswick, the B5289 runs along Derwentwater's eastern shore, providing access to Borrowdale, an idyllic valley characterised by slate-built villages, drystone-walled fields and pockets of ancient woodland, all hemmed in by high, craggy fells. Beyond Seatoller, Borrowdale's last hamlet, the road climbs to cross Honister Pass and then plummets through wild scenery into another spectacular valley, this one containing the lakes of Buttermere and Crummock Water.

The first 11 walks in this book explore the area from Keswick to Buttermere, sampling those atmospheric woods, taking in viewpoints, visiting picturesque villages, following river and lakeshore paths and even climbing to the top of a few low fells.

The landscape to the north and north-west of Keswick is different, with Bassenthwaite Lake occupying the valley bottom while forested slopes lead up to high fells. The final four walks in the book start in this area, initially taking in forest tracks and trails, low felltops and stunning viewpoints before culminating in a single 'challenge route' (Walk 15) that climbs Skiddaw, England's fourth highest mountain.

Most of the routes are circular, but Walks 6 and 7 are linear, making use of bus 78, a regular, year-round service that runs from Keswick to Seatoller through Borrowdale. In addition, the Cat Bells route (Walk 8) uses the Keswick Launch ferry service across Derwentwater to reach the start point at Hawes End.

Where to stay

If you're planning to explore this area of the North Lakes, Keswick makes a great base. There is plenty of accommodation on offer here – from hostels and campsites to B&Bs, inns and hotels – as well as a variety of shops, cafes, pubs, restaurants and, for those wet days, indoor tourist attractions. Braithwaite is popular too, especially with campers, although it has more limited facilities. The same is true of Buttermere, which gets very busy at weekends and during school holidays. If you would like to stay away from the bustle of the main centres, there are accommodation providers and a handful of pubs and cafes scattered throughout Borrowdale and along both sides of Bassenthwaite Lake.

Slightly further afield, you might want to consider basing yourself in Threlkeld or, just outside the National Park, in the lovely town of Cockermouth.

Travel

If you want to leave your car at home, Keswick is the place to aim for. It can be reached by bus from Penrith, which is on the West Coast Main Line railway, with direct trains to Glasgow, Crewe, Manchester, Birmingham and London. Once you've got to Keswick, you'll find that most of the walks in this book can be accessed either directly from the town or by bus – although a few of them rely on seasonal services. The 78 bus runs regularly between Keswick and Seatoller all year round, providing access to all the Borrowdale walks (Walks 3–7). You might also want to download timetables for the 554 and X5 services (Walks 12 and 14). The 77/77A bus starts running in March/April and continues until early November, taking in Braithwaite, Whinlatter, Buttermere and Borrowdale (Walks 1, 2, 8, 12 and 13). For those venturing further afield, the 555 bus opens up opportunities for walking in Windermere, Ambleside and Grasmere, all covered by another book in this series.

Lake cruises are popular, and the Keswick Launch runs throughout the year, stopping at various points around Derwentwater. It can be used in conjunction with several of the walks in this book and is the recommended way to reach the start of the Cat Bells walk (Walk 8).

Local roads become badly congested during school holidays and at weekends. Although car parks are suggested for all but one of the walks, they fill up quickly. This is particularly true of Buttermere, and there is often a queue of traffic snaking along the narrow Borrowdale road too, so consider leaving your car at home or at your holiday base.

The Keswick Launch stops at several jetties around Derwentwater

Ridge path on Rannerdale Knotts

WALK 1
Rannerdale Knotts

Start/finish	*Buttermere village*
Locate	*CA13 9XA ///eyeful.frown.operation*
Cafes/pubs	*Pubs and cafes in Buttermere*
Transport	*Seasonal bus 77/77A*
Parking	*Pay-and-display car parks in village*
Toilets	*In main car park*

Time 3hr
Distance 8km
(5 miles)
Climb 360m

A short, steep climb onto a grassy ridge and a walk down a hidden side valley

Sitting at the foot of mighty Grasmoor and close to the craggy High Stile range, Rannerdale Knotts (355m) might be only a low summit but it can hold its own among these giants. Its ridge, climbed from Buttermere, is a joy to walk. The northern slopes hide a tranquil side valley that hosts a spectacular bluebell display in springtime, and the return path along its southern flank is graced by mesmerising views of Crummock Water.

Looking down on Crummock Water from Rannerdale Knotts

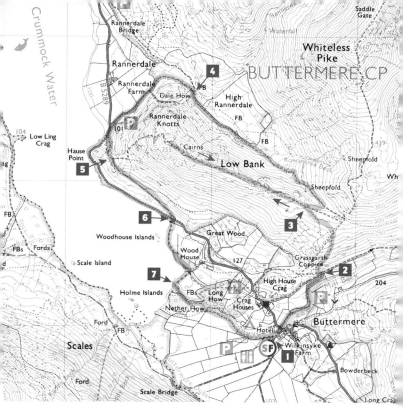

1 With your back to Croft House Farm Cafe in **Buttermere**, turn right. Go left along the B5289 and, almost immediately, go through the gate set back on the right to enter oak woodland. Faced with path choices, always go for the higher option. Leave the woods via a flight of wooden steps and a gate.

2 From the gate, cross diagonally left to pick up a narrow trail heading uphill. Keep right as another trail goes left after just a few strides. At the next path junction, turn right. Bear left at the next fork and then go straight over a crossing of paths. With your first glimpse of Crummock Water ahead, you later step up onto Rannerdale Knotts' grassy ridge path.

3 Bear left along this lovely ridge, negotiating a simple rock step along the way. The highest point on **Rannerdale Knotts** is at the western

The path is fenced to protect the bluebells in Rannerdale

end of the ridge. From the summit, retrace your steps as far as the point at which you first joined the ridge at Waypoint 3. A few metres after passing it, bear left on a narrower path and then left again at the bottom of the drop. Now descend through **Rannerdale**, with Crummock Water straight ahead. The lower reaches of Rannerdale are awash with bluebells in the spring. Nearing the valley's western end, the path goes through a gate.

> Bluebells are normally associated with woodland but can also be found in more open areas such as Rannerdale. The UK is home to about half of the world's bluebells.

4 Turn left immediately after the gate (ignoring the bridge). The path later swings away from the beck. (This section is fenced in spring to protect the bluebells.) Turn left at the road and, in 80m, take the stone-pitched path ascending left. As the gradient eases at the top of the first rise, the path bends to the left.

5 Leave the path on this bend by keeping right along a barely perceptible trail that quickly passes over some rock and becomes more obvious. Bear right at a fork, soon descending

gently on a grass path overlooking **Crummock Water**. Bear right at a fork in the path, dropping to the road.

6 Cross the road, descend the steps and go through a kissing-gate. Walk along the lakeshore as far as some fenced oak woodland. Follow the fence up to the left and enter the woods via a kissing-gate. Dropping back to the lake, cross the bridge and go through the gate to continue along the shore. A small beck is crossed via a bridge a few metres back from the water's edge. Soon after this, go through a kissing-gate at the bottom of **Nether How**, an oak-covered knoll.

7 Turn left after the gate, walking uphill, parallel with the fence on the left. Emerging from the trees, stay close to the fence. When it ends, continue beside the beck. The path becomes more obvious after a gate in a fence. It ends at a gate leading into the main car park at **Buttermere**. Bear left through the car park to return to where the walk started.

> (i) *The Lake District is one of England's last strongholds for the endangered red squirrel, constantly threatened by the incursion of non-native greys.*

An autumn mist hangs over Crummock Water

— To shorten

Descend into Rannerdale from Waypoint 3, missing out the ridge walk to the summit of Rannerdale Knotts. This cuts 50min from the route.

Early tourists

Where Crummock Water laps up at the base of Rannerdale Knotts – at Hause Point – the B5289 has to negotiate a narrow ledge. At the end of the 18th century, when carriages could get no further than this, travellers seeking an alternative to Europe's 'Grand Tour' would take a boat from near the coaching inn at Scale Hill to Low Ling Crag, a narrow spit of land on the west side of the lake. From here, they would walk to Scale Force and on to Buttermere before returning, by boat, to the carriages that awaited them at Hause Point.

Fleetwith towers over the lake

WALK 2
Buttermere circuit

Time 2¼hr
Distance 7km
(4½ miles)
Climb 85m

A straightforward circuit of a small lake surrounded by exquisite mountain scenery

Start/finish	*Buttermere village*
Locate	*CA13 9XA ///eyeful.frown.operation*
Cafes/pubs	*Pubs and cafes in Buttermere*
Transport	*Seasonal bus 77/77A*
Parking	*Pay-and-display car parks in village*
Toilets	*In main car park*

Is this the best lake circuit in the Lake District? Probably! Buttermere is surrounded by high, craggy mountains that rear up ominously from its shores. In the valley itself though, things are more benign. Easy-to-follow paths weave their way in and out of woodland and along the open shore, enabling walkers to relax and enjoy this magnificent landscape. Younger visitors will love the exciting section of unlit rock tunnel.

Pines beside Buttermere

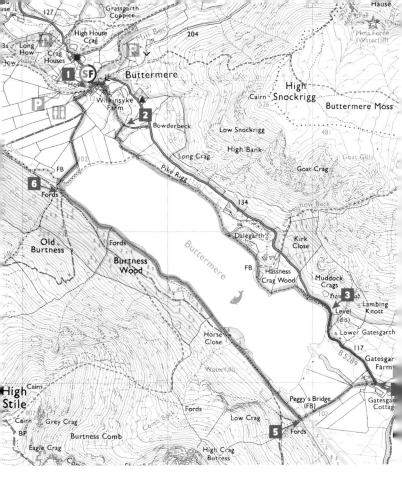

1 With your back to Croft House Farm Cafe in **Buttermere**, turn right and right again along the B5289. In just a few metres, take the track on the right, passing between cottages and farm buildings. About 230m beyond the last building, you reach a gate across the path and a smaller one on the right.

2 Go through the gate on the right. The path soon descends a rocky staircase and bends left. Where a trail drops right, keep left, walking with the lake on your right along the lightly wooded shore, known here as **Pike Rigg**. Enjoy great views of the fells on the other side of the water. These include Red

Looking over Buttermere to Hay Stacks

Pike, High Stile and High Crag. Keep right at any subsequent junctions to stay on the path nearest the water's edge, later passing through a short unlit tunnel in the rocks. Beyond this, the path hugs a small ledge at the base of tree-covered crags. You'll soon be treated to your first uninterrupted view of the fells that crowd the top end of the lake, including Hay Stacks and Fleetwith. Beyond **Hassness Crag Wood**, to stay 'off road' for as long as possible, bear right at a fork as the path begins climbing, but you will eventually reach the road.

3 Stepping up on to the road, simply keep heading in the same direction.

With Fleetwith Edge dominating the scene ahead again, the road drops to **Gatesgarth Farm**.

4 Cross a road bridge near the farm, and immediately turn right through a small gate set back slightly. The path passes to the right of the farm buildings. Don't be tempted by any gates on the right. You soon find yourself on a broad path crossing a flat area a few hundred metres back from the south-eastern end of the lake. Having gone through a few more gates, the path crosses **Peggy's Bridge** over Warnscale Beck to reach another gate.

5 Go through the gate and bear right. This path now heads back along Buttermere's shores. Keep to the clearest route at all times, until you reach a gate at the north-western end of the lake.

In spring, the National Trust closes the permissive paths along Buttermere's north-western shore and at the southern end of neighbouring Crummock Water. This is because sandpipers nest on the shingle beaches here.

6 Go through the gate and cross a bridge. This is quickly followed by a second, more substantial bridge. Walk the clear path with the hedgerow on your left and, at a junction, turn left through the gate. This track now leads back to the village.

ⓘ Many Lake District place names have Norse origins, as do the words 'fell' (for mountain), 'dale' (valley), 'beck' (stream) and 'force' (waterfall).

— To shorten

Walk the northern shore as far as Gatesgarth Farm at Waypoint 4 and then catch the bus (April to November only) back, cutting the walk in half.

The cross on the hill

You might be able to make out a white cross on the rocky ridge, known as Fleetwith Edge, rising almost directly behind Gatesgarth Farm. This is a memorial to Fanny Mercer, a young Victorian woman who fell to her death here after tripping over her walking pole while descending the ridge. The servant of a Rugby schoolmaster, she had been on holiday with her family when the tragic accident happened in September 1887.

WALK 3
Borrowdale, Seathwaite and Seatoller

Time 1¾hr
Distance 5.5km
(3½ miles)
Climb 65m

A gentle
exploration of
woodland and
riverside trails

Start/finish	Seatoller
Locate	CA12 5XN ///uncouth.subplot.consoled
Cafes/pubs	None on route
Transport	Bus 78
Parking	National Trust pay-and-display car park, Seatoller
Toilets	In car park and in Seathwaite

For the first of several walks in Borrowdale, we head to the tiny settlements near the head of the valley, wandering in and out of the gorgeous woods for which the area is justifiably famous and across open pasture at the base of rugged fells. For some of the time, this easy walk follows paths beside the infant River Derwent – Borrowdale's main river.

Autumn in Borrowdale's woods

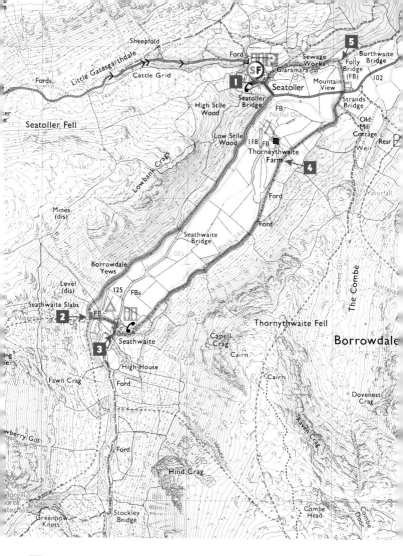

1 From the car park entrance in **Seatoller**, turn left along the road and then take the lane on the right, following it for just over 1km – as far as the bridge over the River Derwent. Before the bridge, go through the gate on the right, signposted for Seathwaite. Beyond a second gate, a path heads upstream beside the river, later passing beneath the **Borrowdale Yews**. The path fords a couple of small becks before reaching a footbridge over Sour Milk Gill.

> The steep slopes to the north of Sour Milk Gill are dotted with spoil heaps, the remains of Borrowdale's 'wad' mines, where graphite was extracted for pencil manufacturing.

2 Cross this footbridge and immediately turn left to cross the gated bridge over the River Derwent. A broad path leads to the farm at **Seathwaite**. After passing through an arch and reaching

the cobbles in front of the cottages, turn right. Drawing level with the far end of the barns, as the main valley track continues ahead towards Stockley Bridge, you'll see a path signposted to Thorneythwaite Farm on the left.

3 Take this path, quickly crossing a bridge and going through a gate. Walk with the wall on your left. After another gate, follow the faint path across this enclosure at the base of **Thornythwaite Fell**. The route ahead becomes more obvious beyond the next gate. After you pass through several more gates, the valley begins to open out and the path becomes more track-like. Follow it as far as a gate near **Thorneythwaite Farm**.

A walker nears Seathwaite

A valley track heads downstream

4 Instead of continuing straight ahead through this gate, the path now swings right. (This is indicated by a sign to the right of the gate.) Walk with the wall on your left at first, and then go through a small gate. Follow the path to a surfaced farm lane and turn right. At the Borrowdale road (B5289), cross over and take the track beside the houses opposite – signposted for Longthwaite. Walking beside the river, go through a gate and keep straight ahead to cross via a stone bridge known as **Folly Bridge**.

5 Once on the north bank of the River Derwent, follow the clear path uphill for a few strides and then take the narrower trail on the left. As you reach a gap in an old wall, go left again, soon entering the woods. When you leave the trees, the path climbs to a gate directly above the Glaramara Hotel. Go through and turn left. Joining a broader path from the right, drop through a gate to return to the car park in **Seatoller**.

> ⓘ *Seathwaite in Borrowdale holds the dubious accolade of being the wettest inhabited place in England, on average receiving over 3550mm of rain annually.*

Cottages at Seatoller

+ To lengthen

From Seathwaite, continue along the main valley track as far as the picturesque Stockley Bridge and then return to Seathwaite to continue on the main route. This adds about 1hr to the walk.

The Borrowdale Yews

The Borrowdale Yews were immortalised in verse by the poet William Wordsworth, who described them as '...those fraternal Four of Borrowdale, joined in one solemn and capacious grove...' There are only three trees left now – the fourth having come down in a storm. Dendrochronology carried out on a branch from the crown of one of the yews revealed it to be 1500 years old, suggesting the trees themselves are several hundred years older.

The walk passes in and out of woodland

WALK 4
Rosthwaite and Stonethwaite

Time 1¼hr
Distance 4.5km (2¾ miles)
Climb 30m

A leisurely stroll up one of Borrowdale's side valleys, taking in two picturesque settlements

Start/finish	Rosthwaite
Locate	CA12 5XB ///slogged.informer.chilled
Cafes/pubs	Pubs and tearoom in Rosthwaite
Transport	Bus 78
Parking	National Trust pay-and-display car park, Rosthwaite
Toilets	Beside car park

The first of three walks starting from the tiny village of Rosthwaite, this route heads into the side valley that is home to the even tinier settlement of Stonethwaite. Slate-built cottages and white-washed farmhouses are encountered beneath towering fells, as we then make our way along quiet lanes to a path beside the River Derwent.

Reflections in an unusually calm Stonethwaite Beck

1 With your back to the car park entrance in **Rosthwaite**, turn left along the lane and left again at the T-junction with the B5289. Take the lane on the right and turn right after the bridge, following the lower path which shadows **Stonethwaite Beck**. The path allows occasional views higher into this side valley, with Eagle Crag prominent on the south-west bank. About 300m after going through the second gate across the track, there is a broad path on the right – signposted Stonethwaite.

2 Turn right at this path junction, soon crossing a footbridge. The path emerges on a lane in **Stonethwaite**.

ⓘ *The Bob Graham Round, named after a Keswick hotelier, is one of Lakeland's most famous fell-running challenges. The 106km circuit involves about 8200m of ascent.*

Turn right and follow the lane to its junction with the B5289. Go straight across, taking the lane opposite. This bends left and crosses a humpback bridge over the **River Derwent**.

3 Turn right immediately after the bridge. As this rough track swings left beyond a white-washed cottage, keep straight ahead, through a gate

Eagle Crag

The route crosses the River Derwent on an old stone bridge

on a riverside path. Cross a wooden footbridge over a tributary beck along the way, then come to a stone bridge (**New Bridge**) on the right.

4 Cross New Bridge and turn right along the track. This track soon bends left and makes its way between the fields to **Rosthwaite**. The car park is on the left about 110m beyond the Flock In tearoom.

Borrowdale's walled enclosures are grazed by Herdwicks, the hardy native sheep that can be seen on some fells all year round. They are born black, turn brown

after about a year and then go grey as they get older.

+ To lengthen

Ignore the right turn at Waypoint 2 and continue upstream for a further 1.4km, as far as the next footbridge (near Smithymire Island). Cross and then head up into Langstrath, crossing the beck via the next bridge and walking back down the track to Stonethwaite. In total, this adds about 1hr 15min.

Cuckoos

Visit Borrowdale in the spring and you'll probably hear cuckoos calling. The birds arrive in the UK in April and usually leave in June. There's no need for them to hang around – they have no young to feed and raise. Instead they lay their eggs in the nests of other birds, which raise the chick thinking it is one of their own. So, at the first opportunity, the cuckoo flies back to Africa and warmer climes.

(i) *Canon Hardwicke Rawnsley, vicar of Crosthwaite, Keswick, was one of the co-founders of the National Trust, set up in 1895.*

Good paths lead through the trees

WALK 5
Castle Crag

Start/finish	Rosthwaite
Locate	CA12 5XB ///slogged.informer.chilled
Cafes/pubs	Pubs and tearoom in Rosthwaite
Transport	Bus 78
Parking	National Trust pay-and-display car park, Rosthwaite
Toilets	Beside car park

Time 2¼hr
Distance 7km (4¼ miles)
Climb 270m

After wandering in and out of riverside woodland, climb steeply to the top of a low fell with magnificent views

The densely wooded Castle Crag sits in the Jaws of Borrowdale, at the point where the valley narrows and higher fells dominate. Its 290m summit, the lowest of all the Wainwrights, is approached from Rosthwaite via woodland and riverside paths where there's a chance of spotting deer and other wildlife. The steep climb to the top is rougher, involving a trail up through slate quarrying waste, but the effort is rewarded with superb views.

Looking down on Borrowdale's fields and cottages

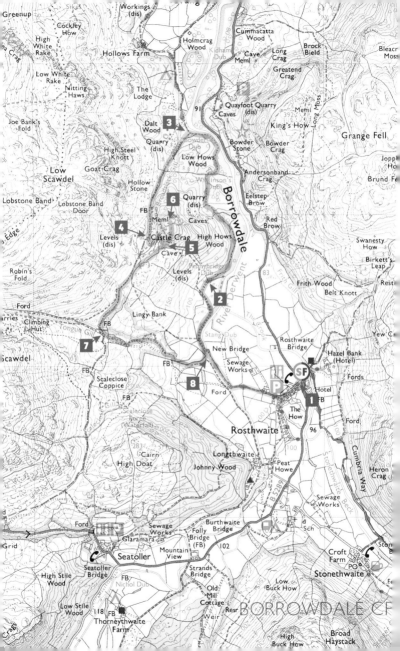

1 With your back to the car park entrance in **Rosthwaite**, turn right along the lane and then keep to the track, eventually crossing **New Bridge** over the River Derwent. Turn right and you'll soon see two gates ahead. Go through the one on the right to continue on the riverside path for now. About 250m beyond the gate, the path swings away from the water and reaches a gate at the woodland edge.

2 Go through the kissing-gate to enter the woods at the base of Castle Crag. After an area of quarry caves and piles of slate, the path splits. Bear right, quickly climbing to a junction where you turn right again. In a further 400m, the woodland path drops back towards the river. Beyond the next gate, descend to a junction of paths

close to where **Broadslack Gill** enters the River Derwent.

3 Turn left at this junction. The small beck is on your right at first, but you then cross it via a small bridge. Leave the woods via a gate and enter a shattered landscape of quarry waste and boulders. Take some time to turn around and enjoy the fantastic views of Derwentwater and Skiddaw behind. About 450m beyond the gate, at a brief lull in the ascent, watch for a faint grassy path on the left.

4 Take this path which soon becomes a clearer, stony route. It quickly doubles back on itself. Go through a gap in a wall, climbing steeply. Once through the next gate, walk beside the fence on the right. At

New Bridge crosses the River Derwent near Rosthwaite

Rosthwaite is full of attractive cottages like this one

a split in the path at the fence corner, bear right. You'll soon see a ladder stile hiding behind a tree trunk.

5 Just before this ladder stile, swing up to the left on the stony path to reach a cairn at the bottom of some quarry workings. Follow the zig-zag path steeply up through the spoil heap. The slate is relatively stable but is slippery when wet. You emerge on a flat area with superb views of Borrowdale. A path to the left explores the quarry workings, but our route continues straight ahead, uphill over exposed tree roots and onto the top of **Castle Crag**.

In 1920, Sir William Hamer bought Castle Crag and gave it to the National Trust in memory of his son Second Lieutenant John Hamer and local men who had been killed during World War 1.

The memorial on Castle Crag

6 Once you've soaked up the views, retrace your steps to the ladder stile at Waypoint 5. (Be aware that this is the lower of two ladder stiles in this wall.) Cross the stile. Immediately, a step stile on the right gives access to a trail beside a fence. Just before this fence

(i) *The Lake District is the second largest National Park in the UK, the largest being the Cairngorms.*

reaches a rock face, the route plummets right. It rejoins the bridleway you followed earlier up Broadslack Gill, but at a higher point. Turn left along this bridleway. In 150m, bear left at a way-marked fork. Cross the bridges over **Tongue Gill** and then, 55m beyond the gate, reach a crossing of paths.

7 Turn left at this junction, dropping through a gate to join a rough track. Soon after passing a ladder stile on the right, the track appears to end. When this happens, swing left to pick up the continuing track. Bear right when it splits. When the track ends, continue downhill on grass, with the beck over to your left. Go through a pedestrian gate beside the beck and over a small footbridge. A faint trail continues downstream with the beck and then goes through another pedestrian gate to reach a clearer path.

8 Turn left at this T-junction, crossing the wooden footbridge and then continuing to New Bridge over the River Derwent. Retracing your steps from earlier, cross the bridge and follow the track back to **Rosthwaite**.

✛ To lengthen

Instead of descending to Rosthwaite at Waypoint 7, continue along the fell-side bridleway for another 1km, descend to Seatoller and then catch the 78 bus back to the start. This adds about 15min to the walk.

The caveman of Castle Crag

Between the two world wars, the quarry caves in the woods on Castle Crag became the summer home of a former insurance clerk called Millican Dalton. Sick of being a commuter in southern England, he migrated north to the Lake District on an annual basis, making ends meet by leading walking parties on the fells and making tents and rucksacks. He turned one cave into a living area and one into a bedroom.

Ashness Gate jetty near the end of the walk

WALK 6
Watendlath and Ashness Bridge

Start	Rosthwaite
Locate	CA12 5XB ///slogged.informer.chilled
Finish	Bus stop outside Derwentwater Hostel on B5289
Cafes/pubs	Pubs and tearoom in Rosthwaite, tearoom in Watendlath (100m off route)
Transport	Bus 78
Parking	National Trust pay-and-display car park, Rosthwaite
Toilets	Beside car park at start and in Watendlath

Time 2½hr
Distance 7.5km
(4¾ miles)
Climb 320m

A slightly harder, linear walk visiting beauty spots above Borrowdale

A secluded tarnside hamlet, a hanging valley, oak woods, a 'surprise' view and a photogenic bridge with a mountain backdrop are just some of the highlights on this varied linear walk above Borrowdale. Add in a choice of pubs and cafes, as well as a return bus ride through this most beautiful of valleys, and you've got all the makings of a great day out.

Signposted path junction above Rosthwaite

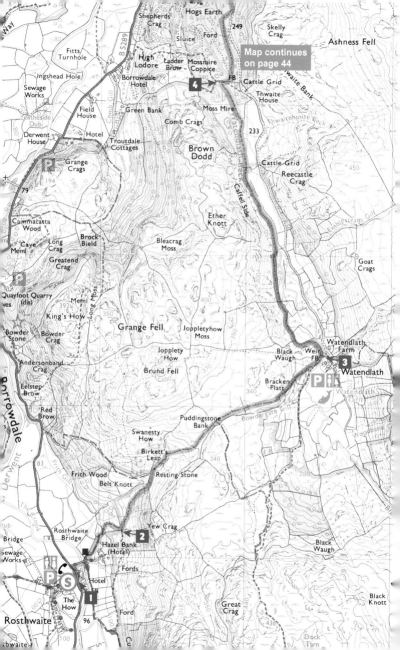

Map continues on page 44

1 With your back to the car park entrance in **Rosthwaite**, turn left along the lane and left again at the T-junction with the B5289. Take the lane on the right and turn left after the bridge. The clear path narrows as it passes to the right of a private parking area and soon begins climbing to reach a gate.

2 After the gate at the top of the first climb, turn left along a clear but rough track. This leads all the way to a humpback bridge on the edge of **Watendlath**.

> Watendlath was the last place in the Lake District to get mains electricity, in 1978. Connected to the main dale by a narrow, lane, it still has an isolated feel about it.

3 The route doesn't cross the bridge to enter the hamlet, but you may wish to make the short detour to explore or visit the tearoom The main route goes through the gate beside the bridge and follows the path for just over 2km along the hanging valley occupied by **Watendlath Beck**, until it reaches another bridge over the beck.

4 Cross this bridge and then go through the gate in the wall on your left. A clear path now leads through **Ashness Woods** to a minor road along which you turn left.

> About 280m along the road, you reach 'Surprise View', partly concealed from the road by the trees. Stepping off the asphalt to the left reveals a flawless panorama

Watendlath Beck in autumn

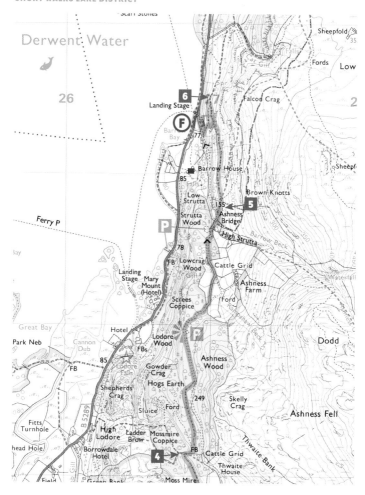

which includes Cat Bells, Skiddaw and Derwentwater. Be careful as you peer over the edge – the ground falls away steeply.

Continue down the road for another 800m to **Ashness Bridge**. With Skiddaw forming the perfect mountain backdrop, this old humpback

Ashness Bridge

bridge is probably one of the most photographed places in the Lakes.

5 Soon after crossing Ashness Bridge, watch for a fingerpost to the right of the road. Take the narrow footpath here – signposted Great Wood. It briefly runs parallel with the road, but then swings up to a gate. Once through this, keep left at an early fork. About 650m after leaving the road, having passed through a lightly wooded area, the path splits. Bearing left, you find yourself on a small rock outcrop overlooking Derwentwater.

6 Turn sharp left from the rock outcrop, almost back on yourself, following what is at first a faint path. The trail drops to the Watendlath lane, where

you turn right. Turn left along the B5289 beside **Derwentwater**. The bus stop for your ride back to Rosthwaite is at the entrance to the Derwentwater Hostel – on the left in 150m.

— To shorten

From Ashness Bridge at Waypoint 5, continue downhill on the lane to the junction with the B5289, cutting 10min off the walk.

ⓘ *The Lake District's oak woods are remnants of the immense forests that once cloaked Europe's Atlantic coast, all the way from Portugal to Norway.*

In the woods along Derwentwater's western shore

WALK 7
Derwentwater shore

Time 2½hr
Distance 9.5km
(6 miles)
Climb 110m

A long but easy
walk in and out
of woodland
and beside the
lake, finishing at
Keswick

Start	*Bus stop on B5289 near Grange*
Locate	*CA12 5XA ///blending.afraid.lotteries*
Finish	*Bus stands in front of Booths super-market, Keswick*
Cafes/pubs	*Cafes in Grange and Portinscale, pubs and cafes in Keswick*
Transport	*Bus 78*
Parking	*Use one of Keswick's car parks and catch bus to start point*
Toilets	*In Grange and in the Bell Close and Lakeside car parks in Keswick*

Walkers can catch the bus from Keswick to start
this route at Borrowdale's quiet riverside village
of Grange. After a short stretch of road walking,
it heads for Derwentwater. Once you reach the
lake, good paths take you north along the open
shore and through mixed woodland. All the
while, breathtaking views of Skiddaw come and
go. The routes passes several cafes and through
the village of Portinscale on its way to Keswick. It
is also possible to cut the walk short by catching
the Keswick Launch from one of the five piers on
this side of the lake.

Derwentwater and Skiddaw

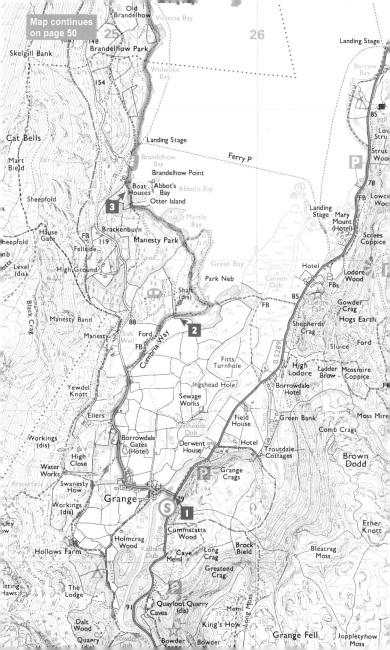

Map continues
on page 50

25

26

Old
Brandelhow

Victoria Bay

Landing Stage

Skelgill Bank

Brandelhow Park

148

Barrow
Bay

154

Witheside Bay

85

Cat Bells

Landing Stage

Low
Stru

Mart
Bield

Brandelhow
Bay

Ferry P

Strut
Woo

Brandelhow Point

P

Sheepfold

Boat
Houses

Abbot's
Bay

Abbot's Bay

78

3

Otter Island

FB

Lowe
Woo

Hause
Gate

FB

Brackenburn

Myrtle
Bay

Landing
Stage

Screes
Coppice

heepfold

119

Fellside

Mary
Mount
(Hotel)

Level
(dis)

High Ground

Manesty Park

Great Bay

Hotel

Lodore
Wood

ots

Park Neb

Cannon
Dub

FBs

Gowder
Crag

Black Crag

Manesty Band

Shaft
(dis)

85

Lodore
Falls

Hogs Earth

Manesty

88

Salt
Well

Ford

Cumbria Way

2

FB

FB

Shepherds
Crag

Sluice

Ford

Yewdel
Knott

Fitts
Turnhole

80

High
Lodore

Ladder
Brow

Mossmire
Coppice

Ellers

Ingshead Hole

Borrowdale
Hotel

Moss Mire

Workings
(dis)

Eathside
Dub

Sewage
Works

Field
House

Green Bank

Comb Crags

Water
Works

High
Close

Borrowdale
Gates
(Hotel)

Derwent
House

Hotel

Troutdale
Cottages

Brown
Dodd

Waterfall

Swanesty
How

P

Grange
Crags

enup

Workings
(dis)

Grange

S

79

1

194

Ether
Knott

ky

Holmcrag
Wood

Kidham
Dub

Cave
Meml

Long
Crag

Brock
Bield

Bleacrag
Moss

Hollows Farm

Greatend
Crag

Meml

The
Lodge

91

Quayfoot Quarry
Caves

(dis)

Meml

King's How

Grange Fell

Joppletyhow
Moss

Dalt
Wood

Quarry

tting
laws

Bowder

Bowder

1 From the bus stop on the B5289, cross the River Derwent road bridge and walk through **Grange**. After just over 1km of road walking, turn right through a gate onto a clear path – signposted Lodore. Beyond a kissing-gate, a larger gate provides access to heathland near Derwentwater's southern tip.

2 After going through the larger gate, keep right and bear right again after a short section of boardwalk. Turn left on reaching the surfaced path near the shore of **Derwentwater**. Beyond a gate in a dry-stone wall, you enter woodland. These woods formed part of the National Trust's first Lake District acquisition, bought by public subscription in 1902 to prevent housing development. On reaching a narrow lane at a cottage, turn right, soon reaching a fork.

3 Bear left at this fork and then, just after the next cottage, descend the rough slope on the right to go through a gate near the water's edge. The path hugs the lakeshore and then re-enters woods. Bear right at a fork to drop to the **landing stage** at High Brandelhow.

> Tired walkers can catch the boat back to Keswick from this pier or from one of four others along this side of the lake. Stand at the far end of the jetty a few minutes before the launch is due – otherwise the boat will not stop.

At the next landing stage – Low Brandelhow – go through the gate.

4 Turn left after the gate. Having ignored a path to Hawse End jetty, turn right along a surfaced lane and then keep right in front of **Hawes End**

The Keswick Launch on Derwentwater

Boats at Nichol End Marine

Outdoor Centre. A few metres after passing another path signposted to Hawes End jetty, there is a small gate on the right.

5 Go through the gate. After an open area, go straight over a rough track. At a lane near the entrance to Lingholm, cross diagonally left to continue on the path towards Keswick – beside the wall and then a fence on the right. Having crossed one more surfaced lane, drop into the car park for **Nichol End Marine**. Turn left along the driveway and follow it to the road.

6 Turn right at the road. As it bends left in **Portinscale**, take the lane on the right. At the end of this, cross the

suspension bridge and, after 100m, turn right along a fenced path between fields. Turn left on reaching a lane and then go right at the main road through Keswick. Turn right at the mini-roundabout. When the road bends left, keep right and the bus stands are on the right, in front of Booths supermarket.

– To shorten

Catch the boat back to Keswick from one of five Keswick Launch jetties – High Brandelhow, Low Brandelhow, Hawse End, Lingholm and Nichol End – reducing the walk by up to 1hr 40min.

Derwentwater is the National Park's third largest lake

Mining heritage

Look around as you wander through Borrowdale and beside Derwentwater, and you'll see evidence of the area's mining history – spoil heaps, fenced shafts, open adits on the fellside, abandoned buildings…These scars have almost all been created since 1564, the year Elizabeth I invited the Germans, at that time the best miners in Europe, to England to help her find the metals she so desperately needed, including copper. To find out more about the area's history, drop in on the exhibitions at Grange Methodist Church and St Andrew's, Stonethwaite.

WALK 8
Cat Bells

Start/finish	Hawes End jetty
Locate	CA12 5TP ///materials.fitter.summit
Cafes/pubs	None on route
Transport	From Keswick, catch Keswick Launch to start point. Alternatively, in summer, the 77/77A bus stops near Waypoint 2
Parking	Lakeside pay-and-display car park in Keswick
Toilets	In car park

Time 2¾hr
Distance 6.5km (4 miles)
Climb 450m

A boat trip is followed by a stiff, sometimes rocky climb to a popular viewpoint

A 10-minute ride on the Keswick Launch to Hawse End is followed by a climb onto Cat Bells, one of the finest viewpoints in the area. The climb is steep in places and involves clambering on bare rock. After dropping from the ridge, the return route uses an easy-going terrace path along the base of the fell, providing a second, more leisurely opportunity to drink in those wonderful lake and fell views.

The return route uses a terrace path along the base of Cat Bells

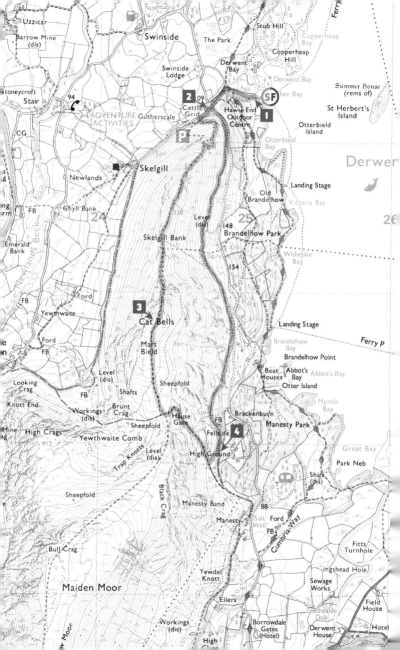

1 Step off the Hawse End jetty and keep straight ahead, walking with the water and then a fence on your right. After a gate, a clear path leads to the access lane for **Hawes End Outdoor Centre**. Turn right here and, almost immediately, take the path climbing left to a road.

2 Turn left at the road, go through the pedestrian gate at the top of a few steps and take the right-hand path. Rejoining the road, cross over, take a few strides to the right and then climb the steps on your left – signposted Cat Bells summit. This path soon joins another coming up from the right. As the main route swings right at a fork to begin climbing the ridge, Derwentwater and its many islands appear. At the first rocky section, it is best to head left to avoid polished, slippery rock. Soon after this, the going gets a little easier for a short while. The path then dips slightly before climbing again – at an even steeper angle than before. This section involves one short, easy rock clamber, and, once you've surmounted this difficulty, the summit of **Cat Bells** is only a few metres further on.

From the top, you can see that there are four islands on Derwentwater. The largest is St Herbert's Island which became 'Owl Island' in Beatrix Potter's *The Tale of Squirrel Nutkin*.

Views across the Newlands Valley on the climb up

Viewfinder on Cat Bells

3 From the top, continue in the same direction along the stony ridge path. When this drops to a junction in the dip (hause) between Cat Bells and Maiden Moor, fork left. Ignore any shortcut trails on the left – most of these are blocked off to prevent further erosion of these slopes – until you reach an obvious fork. Bear left here to descend some more stone steps and drop to the terrace path above the buildings at **Manesty**.

4 Turn left here to skirt the eastern base of Cat Bells. While the slopes on the right drop to Derwentwater, Skiddaw is the most dominant feature ahead, with Blencathra to the north-east. The path briefly drops to the road but immediately continues on the far side of this tiny layby.

Ignoring any trails to the left, you'll drop back to this road 1.5km beyond the layby. Cross the road diagonally left and descend some steps. After a gate, retrace your steps from earlier by turning right along the road. Remember to turn right again on the bend, fork right on the path, turn right along Hawes End centre's access lane and then go through the gap in the railings on the left to return to the jetty.

+ To lengthen

Instead of catching the boat or bus to return to Keswick, walk back using Walk 7, joining it at Waypoint 5 near Hawse End jetty. This adds 90min to the walk.

WALK 9
Friar's Crag and Castlehead

Time 2¼hr
Distance 7km
(4¼ miles)
Climb 230m

**Classic lake
views and an
optional climb to
a breathtaking
viewpoint**

Start/finish	*Lakeside car park, Lake Road, Keswick*
Locate	*CA12 5DJ ///corrupted.snails.decades*
Cafes/pubs	*Cafe at Theatre by the Lake*
Transport	*Keswick is served by buses 78, 554, 555, X4/X5 and, in summer, 77/77A*
Parking	*Lakeside pay-and-display car park*
Toilets	*In car park*

Sparkling Derwentwater and its surrounding fells
dominate this walk. The route starts by heading
along shore paths, taking in much-photographed
views along the way. A climb through the towering
trees of Great Wood provides a bird's-eye perspective
on this fine scene before dropping back towards
Keswick and the opportunity for one final, rough
ascent to yet another viewpoint.

Bench on Friar's Crag

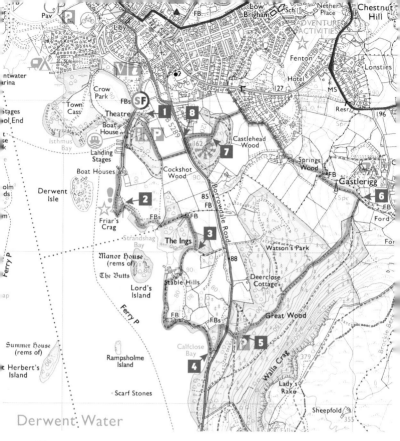

1 Turn left out of the car park to reach the landing stages on Derwentwater. Walk with the lake on your right, keeping right at any junctions to reach the benches at the end of **Friar's Crag**.

Friar's Crag is believed to have been the embarkation point for monks making a pilgrimage to St Herbert's Island on Derwentwater.

St Herbert was a religious recluse who lived here in the 7th century.

2 From the benches, turn round and begin heading back the way you came, but then, almost immediately, take the path on the right, soon passing the Ruskin Monument. The path swings right, through a gate onto the lakeshore. On the far side of this open area, go through another gate to follow the

The 'Hundred Year Stone' on Calfclose Bay

boardwalk through wet woodland to a T-junction.

3 Turn right at this junction, later returning to the lake. The shore path passes through a patch of yew woodland before heading back into the open beside **Calfclose Bay**. Look out for the Hundred Year Stone, a sculpture by the artist Peter Randall-Page, created in 1995 to mark the centenary of the founding of the National Trust. Soon after a tiny bridge, you enter denser woodland.

4 Almost immediately after re-entering the trees, take the path climbing left. Keep straight on as one trail heads right – to a bus stop on the B5289 – but then take the next path on the right to reach the road. Cross the road and

walk up the access lane opposite. Turn left to enter the National Trust car park at **Great Wood**. You'll immediately see a narrow trail heading up the grassy slope straight ahead – signposted Great Wood Walk.

5 Take this trail. Keep right on joining a broader path from the left. Climbing steadily all the while, bear right at the next fork, following the clearer path. As you near the top edge of the woods, ignore a waymarked path to the right and continue to a T-junction of routes.

6 Turn left here. Dropping to another junction near a bridge, turn left and continue to a gate. Go through this and carry on straight ahead, past Springs Farm and on to a quiet, residential street. Almost 500m beyond Springs

Benches and Scots pines on Castlehead

Farm, turn left on to a fenced path – signposted Castlehead and Lake Road. Enter the woods via a gate and bear right. Keep left at an early fork, climbing to a fence corner.

7 From this fence, bear left again to climb to the top of **Castlehead**. The summit, with its benches and view-finder, is just 100m from the main path – and has gorgeous views – but the last part of the ascent is across bare rock and exposed tree roots, so watch your footing. Having visited the top, return to the fence corner and turn left to drop to the **B5289**.

8 Cross the road and turn left along a path on the other side of the hedge. About 50m along this path, descend the steps on the right and walk between two fields. Entering **Cockshot Wood**, turn right and then bear right at a fork to return to the Lakeside car park.

✚ To lengthen

For another perspective on Derwentwater, head into Crow Park for a 20–30min stroll at the end of the walk.

John Ruskin

One of the most influential thinkers of the 19th century, John Ruskin first visited the Lake District when he was five. He once said, 'The first thing I remember as an event in life was being taken by my nurse to the brow of Friar's Crag on Derwentwater'. It was, he continued, 'the creation of the world for me'. Ruskin had a strong desire to improve conditions for the poor, and his ideas had a profound effect on the early development of the Labour Party.

The Ruskin Monument

Castlerigg Stone Circle on a cold winter's morning

WALK 10
Castlerigg Stone Circle

Time 2¼hr
Distance 7.5km (4¾ miles)
Climb 200m

Through woods and across fields to a prehistoric enigma

Start/finish	*Moot Hall, Keswick*
Locate	*CA12 5JR ///dime.epidemics.flies*
Cafes/pubs	*Cafe at Keswick Climbing Wall (150m from stone circle), wide choice in Keswick*
Transport	*Keswick is served by buses 78, 554, 555, X4/X5 and, in summer, 77/77A*
Parking	*Various car parks in Keswick*
Toilets	*Nearest at Bell Close car park, Keswick*

The 5000-year-old stone circle at Castlerigg occupies a magnificent spot, towered over by Blencathra and the northernmost reaches of the Helvellyn range. After following a gently climbing woodland path from the edge of Keswick, this walk heads out across fields to visit the prehistoric site. A quiet road then drops into the town and picks up the route of the old railway.

Views of the northernmost tops of the Helvellyn range

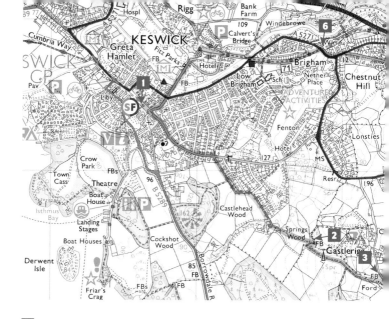

1 With your back to the entrance of Moot Hall information centre, take the lane (the continuation of Main Street) to the left of Greggs. Keep straight ahead along St John's Street. Nearing the edge of town, before the road starts climbing steeply, turn right along Springs Road. Beyond Springs Farm, a rough track passes through a gate and climbs through woodland to a footbridge.

View of Keswick from Spring Road

the gate on the right – signposted Castlerigg Stone Circle.

3 Beyond the gate, walk with a wall on your left across two fields next to the camping field at **Castlerigg Farm**. The hills straight ahead form part of the long ridge extending north from Helvellyn. After a gate, turn left along a rough track. With views now dominated by Skiddaw and Blencathra, the route hugs the left-hand edge of fields to reach the **A591**.

Helvellyn (950m) and Skiddaw (931m) are England's third and fourth highest mountains, respectively. The highest is Scafell Pike (978m), followed closely by its neighbour Scafell (964m).

4 Turn right along the pavement and, in another 100m, go left along the

2 Just before the bridge, turn sharp right, soon climbing more steeply. After a wooden footbridge, climb to a quiet lane. Turn left along this and, almost immediately, go through

Castlerigg Stone Circle

access track for **High Nest**. Pass to the left of the farmhouse and through a gate to the right of a barn conversion. The route follows the field boundary on the right and goes through a small gate. Walk straight across the next field and through a small gate in a wall. Swing slightly left to make for another gate, beyond which you continue parallel with the field boundary to the left. The faint path eases its way up towards the fence on the left and reaches a minor road. Turn left. The field containing **Castlerigg Stone Circle** is on the left in 150m.

5 After visiting the stone circle, return to the road and continue in the same direction as before. Go left at the T-junction on the edge of **Keswick** and right along the A591 for 100m. A gate on the left then provides access to a trail that drops to the surfaced Keswick Railway Path.

6 Turn left along the disused railway. After passing the platform of the former Keswick Railway Station (now a hotel), bear left around the side of the leisure centre. Follow the path around the front of the building and out to the road. Bear right. Go straight over at the busy crossroads, along Station Street. When this bends sharp left, turn right to return to the Moot Hall where you started.

– To shorten

Instead of following field paths from the A591, at Waypoint 4, cross straight over and follow the minor lane (Castle Lane) to a T-junction. Go right and right again to reach the stone circle. This knocks about 10min from the route and is recommended after wet weather.

Mystery of the stones

Comprising about 40 stones, Castlerigg Stone Circle is one of the UK's oldest and best-preserved stone circles. Nobody knows what Neolithic people used it for, although various theories have been put forward. The unearthing, in 1875, of an axe-head led some to suggest it was used as a trading post for these tools, but the stones' alignment with the midwinter sunrise has given rise to other, astronomy-based theories. Whatever the reason for its construction, it remains an atmospheric location.

WALK 11
Latrigg and Keswick Railway Path

Time 3hr
Distance 9.5km (6 miles)
Climb 320m

Start/finish	Keswick Leisure Centre
Locate	CA12 4NE ///immune.longer.assemble
Cafes/pubs	Wide choice in Keswick
Transport	Keswick is served by buses 78, 554, 555, X4/X5 and, in summer, 77/77A
Parking	Keswick Leisure Centre car park
Toilets	Nearest at Bell Close car park, Keswick

A short climb to a popular felltop, returning to Keswick via a disused railway

Crouching at the base of Skiddaw, Latrigg is an easily reached vantage point from which to gaze down on Derwentwater and across to the high fells beyond. It's a steady climb from Keswick. Then, having reached the top and walked the broad, grassy summit ridge, drop to the River Greta as it passes through a gorge for a gentle return via a disused railway.

One of many bridges on the Keswick Railway Path

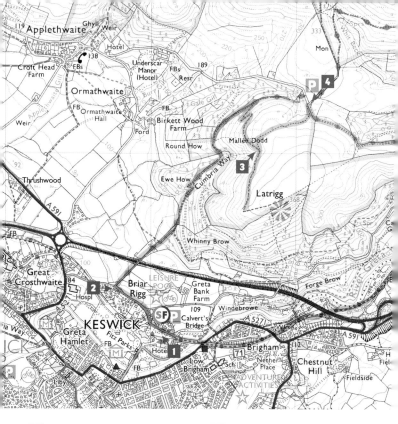

1 Leave the leisure centre car park via the mini-roundabout at its main entrance. The route now goes left along Brundholme Road, but uses a footpath to the right of the road. This provides a safer alternative to walking the road itself. It crosses straight over one minor road along the way. About 550m beyond the roundabout, watch for a broad track – signposted Skiddaw – on the right.

2 Take this track. After a road bridge and then a gate, it climbs beside Brundholme Wood. When the trees allow, you'll see Skiddaw straight ahead. Ignore all paths to the right as you climb. When the track swings around the northern flank of Latrigg, there is a fence on the left. Ignoring a gate in the fence, keep right here. Take the next path on the right – signposted Latrigg summit – almost heading back on yourself. The path zig-zags its way

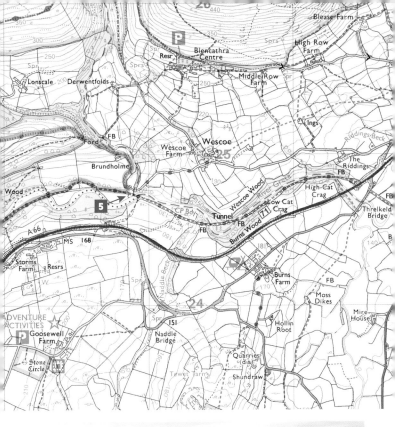

Winter walkers climbing Latrigg

Keswick and Derwentwater seen from the top

steadily uphill, eventually joining another path from the left.

3 Keep right at this junction. A bench near the summit of **Latrigg** soon provides somewhere to rest and admire the fantastic views – over Keswick and Derwentwater and across to the Newlands and Coledale fells. The unmarked true summit, 200m further on, can be reached by following the path round to the left. From the bench, return to the junction at Waypoint 3 and keep right. Drop to a path junction near a parking area.

4 Turn right along the track, hugging the northern base of Latrigg and later descending through gorse. Gorse is unusual in that it can flower at any time of year. On warm days, the coconut-like scent of its distinctive yellow blooms fills the air. After a gate and stile, a lane is reached. Turn left here and follow the lane down to the right, into the valley bottom. At the bottom of the drop, and just before the lane crosses the Glenderaterra Beck, go through the gate on the right. A path leads to another gate.

5 Go through the gate and turn right along the railway path. It's hard to go wrong now – this clear, wide, mostly level track takes you all the way back to Keswick, crossing and recrossing the **River Greta** via several bridges and passing through a lit tunnel along the way. It ends at the car park where the walk started, close to the platform of the former Keswick Railway Station (now a hotel).

+ To lengthen

To see more of the old railway, turn left at Waypoint 5 and walk as far as the A66. Then return to Waypoint 5 to rejoin the route described above. This adds about 1hr to the walk.

Keswick Railway Path

The Keswick to Threlkeld Railway Path uses the bed of the former 31-mile Cockermouth, Keswick and Penrith line, built by Thomas Bouch in 1865. It brought coke from the Durham coal mines to the iron-making industry on the west coast. It was closed in 1972, but

later gained a new lease of life as a shared cycleway and footpath.

The Keswick Railway Path passes through a long tunnel

Derwentwater from the ridge path

WALK 12
Barrow

Start/finish	*Royal Oak pub, Braithwaite*
Locate	*CA12 5SY ///puzzle.piston.seriously*
Cafes/pubs	*Pubs and coffee house in Braithwaite*
Transport	*Buses X5 and, in summer, 77/77A*
Parking	*Village school car park can be used outside of school hours, or park on roadside nearby*
Toilets	*No public toilets on route*

Time 2¼hr
Distance 5km
(3¼ miles)
Climb 380m

A short, steep climb followed by superb ridge walking on a low fell

Braithwaite, near Keswick, is surrounded by an impressive array of fells, many of which are more than 750m in altitude. This walk isn't about climbing those high, craggy fells, but it does provide a considerable sense of achievement. The 455m top of Barrow is reached via some enjoyable ridge walking in magnificent surroundings.

The walk starts from Braithwaite

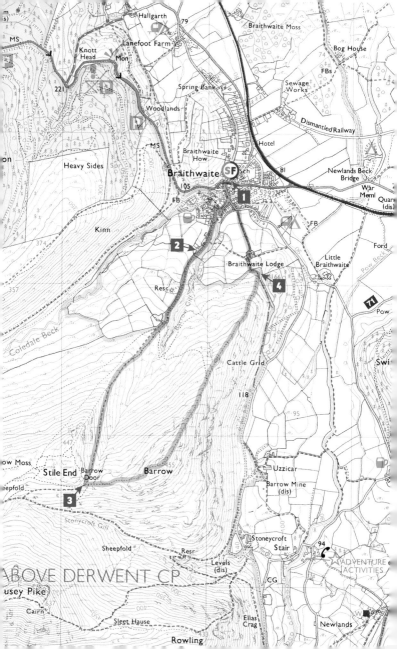

Grisedale Pike watches over grazing ewes

1 Standing beside the B5292 in **Braithwaite** with your back to the Royal Oak, turn left then left again down a narrow lane between buildings. After the bridge over **Coledale Beck**, take the road on the right (but not sharp right along the beckside lane). At a T-junction, go left and follow the lane until it ends at a gate.

2 Go through the gate to access a track. Ignoring tracks to the right – as well as narrower trails to the left – continue straight ahead. The stone track later becomes a broad, grassy swathe through the bracken. Follow it up through the narrowing valley until you reach a junction of paths at **Barrow Door**, the gap between Barrow and Stile End.

3 Turn left to begin the climb onto **Barrow**. With rock underfoot at times, the route splits on the way up. It doesn't matter which option you take but keep to the path to avoid adding to the erosion scars. From the summit, descend the other side of the ridge. Keep to the mostly grassy apex until you drop off the fell's north-eastern end and reach a T-junction with another broad, grassy path.

The remains of Force Crag mine are visible on Grisedale Pike on the opposite side of Coledale. Various minerals were extracted in this area from Elizabethan times until the 1990s, including lead, zinc and barytes.

Skiddaw fills the view ahead as you descend from Barrow's summit

4 Turn left at this junction. Beyond a small gate, drop through a wooden farm gate and walk between the outbuildings of **Braithwaite Lodge**. Swing right and then left along the access track. Turn left when you reach the road. Follow it through the village and over the bridge you crossed at the start of the walk. The Royal Oak is on your right as you reach the **B5292**.

✚ To lengthen

After Waypoint 2, instead of following the clear path all the way to Barrow Door, climb the ridge on the right to the top of Stile End and then drop from here to Barrow Door, adding about 15min to the walk.

Pencil manufacturing

Pencil manufacturing began in the Keswick area after graphite, known locally as wad, was discovered in Borrowdale in the 16th century. The Cumberland Pencil Company, established in the mid-19th century to commercially exploit the graphite, was originally located in Braithwaite. It moved to Keswick in 1898 after the Braithwaite mill was destroyed by fire. In 2008 the firm moved to nearby Workington, but Keswick remains home to a museum dedicated to all things pencil.

WALK 13

Seat How and the Whinlatter forests

Start/finish	*Whinlatter Visitor Centre*
Locate	*CA12 5TW ///challenge.excavate.aims*
Cafes/pubs	*Cafe at visitor centre*
Transport	*Bus 77/77A (summer only)*
Parking	*Pay-and-display at visitor centre*
Toilets	*At visitor centre*

Seat How is an excellent little viewpoint, poking its treeless head above the forests of Whinlatter to gaze out to the imposing fells surrounding it. This walk climbs to the 496m summit, using the forest's network of waymarked tracks and trails. There is a moderate amount of ascent, but the climbs are well spaced out, with only one or two short steep stretches. Whinlatter Forest is also popular with mountain bikers – some trails are pedestrian-only, but most are shared use.

Time 2¼hr
Distance 6km (3¾ miles)
Climb 260m

Follow forest trails up to a low top poking its head above the trees

Path junction with view of Grisedale Pike

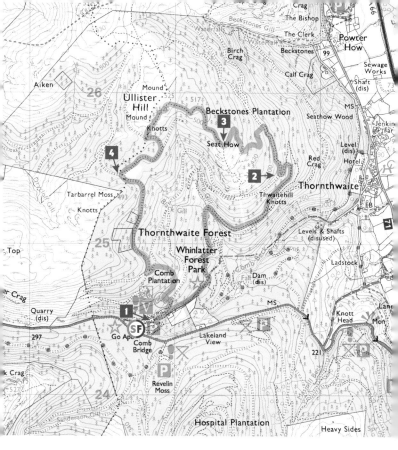

1 Standing on the car park access lane directly below the **visitor centre**, with your back to the building, turn left. Keep right at the fork as you draw level with the Cyclewise bike hire shop. Having ignored any lesser trails along the way, you reach a clear fork in the track. Bear left to begin your uphill journey. On reaching a bench near **Thwaitehill Knotts**, with a superb bird's-eye perspective on Keswick, keep left along the broader, rising track. The imposing bulk of Skiddaw can be glimpsed from time to time, but the tree cover means these sightings are brief. When the incline steepens and the track bends left, another path joins from the right. In a further 100m, you reach another junction, with way-marker post number 9 on the right.

The path leading up towards Seat How

2 Turn right at waymarker post 9 and, in another 400m, watch for post 54 to the left. Leaving the more popular forest tracks, take the narrow, but clear and bike-free path rising behind this. It winds its way up through the trees, crossing straight over the Altura mountain bike trail at the base of **Seat How**. Bear left at the next waymarker post to reach the bare summit of the hill. Seat How is exposed to the wind, but exposed also to some impressive views that include Grisedale Pike, Derwentwater and Skiddaw.

3 From the top of Seat How, return to the last waymarker post and then keep straight ahead. The trail meanders through the trees in somewhat disorientating manner, reaching the uppermost edge of the forest and then dropping to a slightly wider path at waymarker post 53. Turn left here. Having joined a path from the left, continue to the next junction – beside post number 3 at **Tarbarrel Moss**.

4 Turn left at this junction. On dropping to a bench at a more open area (with picnic tables below), follow the track round to the left and, almost immediately, take the bike-free route on the right. At a trail junction, go straight over, passing behind a line of benches. Keep right when the route quickly splits. Reaching a play area, follow the broad path round to the left and then turn right along a forest track. When you draw level with the Cyclewise shop, keep straight ahead to retrace your steps to the **visitor centre**.

Picnic area with a view of the Helvellyn range

▬ To shorten

Bear left at Waypoint 2 and, having ignored one turning on the left after 350m, continue for another 1km and then fork left to descend slowly to the visitor centre. This reduces the walk by about 45min.

ⓘ *Yew, juniper and Scots pine are the only conifers native to the UK. All can be found in the Lake District.*

Trench warfare

Forestry England visitor centre at Whinlatter

Since the outbreak of World War 1, the country had been unable to rely on timber imports and had struggled to meet demand – with trench warfare placing particular pressure on resources. As a result, the state-run Forestry Commission (now Forestry England) was set up to oversee reafforestation. Whinlatter was the site of the Forestry Commission's first Lake District plantations – in 1919.

Memorial stone on the summit of Dodd

WALK 14
Dodd

Start/finish	Dodd Wood car park
Locate	CA12 4QD ///flicks.motive.broadens
Cafes/pubs	Tearoom in car park
Transport	Buses 554 and X5
Parking	Forestry England's Dodd Wood pay-and-display car park on A591, 6.5km (4 miles) north of Keswick
Toilets	In car park

Time 2¼hr
Distance 5.5km (3½ miles)
Climb 400m

A steep forest hike to a viewpoint high above the trees, and a chance of spotting ospreys

Squatting at the foot of mighty Skiddaw, Dodd is just a tiny pimple on England's fourth highest mountain, but for walkers it's a rewarding spot. The short, sharp pull up through Dodd Wood leads to a summit that provides tremendous views of this corner of the Lake District and across the water into Scotland. Visit from April to August, and there's also a chance of spotting the ospreys that nest near Bassenthwaite Lake.

Old Sawmill Tearoom

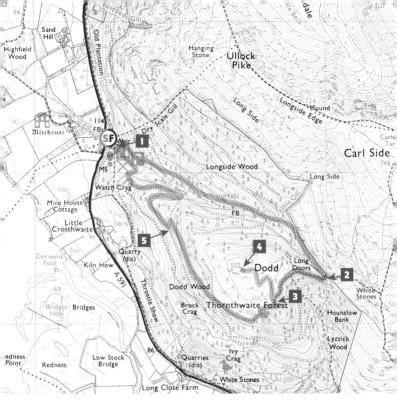

Cross the footbridge behind the Old Sawmill Tearoom and head uphill on the path, ignoring an early turning to the left. On reaching a surfaced forest path, turn right, climbing fairly steeply. Ignore a red and green-marked trail dropping right to cross Skill Beck. As you make your way uphill, the tall conifers give way to deciduous species dominated by beech. As you near the forest's top edge, another track joins from the left. The route briefly levels off and

another track then joins from the right, followed in 100m by a path up to the right, with a green Dodd summit trail marker beside it.

2 Turn right up the summit trail. Your first two rewards for the earlier, tiring climb come almost immediately – a wonderful view of Derwentwater and a handy bench from which to enjoy it. Ascending again, you reach another green waymarker post where a narrow trail is indicated to the left.

The walk starts from a bridge behind the cafe

3 This junction marks the start of your return route later in the walk, but for now stick with the main path as it swings sharp right. It winds its way to the summit of **Dodd**, topped by a tall memorial stone, with views down to Bassenthwaite Lake and beyond. On a clear day, looking north-west you might spot the hills on the Scottish side of the Solway Firth.

There are lots of lakes in the Lake District, but only one has the word 'lake' in its name – and that is Bassenthwaite Lake. The others are called 'meres' or 'waters'.

Bassenthwaite Lake from the summit

View along Bassenthwaite Lake

4 Tearing yourself away from the view, retrace your steps as far as the narrow, green-waymarked trail at Waypoint 3. Turn right here. Just before another well-placed bench, turn right again along an even narrower path heading downhill. The route re-enters the trees before traversing the fellside high above **Bassenthwaite Lake**. This is a lovely stretch of path – you can really stride out as you take in the views glimpsed through the trees. After a left bend, the path drops to a wide track.

5 Turn right along the track. At the next junction high above **Skill Beck**, turn left. Take the first turning on the right, following green and red waymarkers downhill. Descending to another path junction, turn sharp right – still with the green and red trails. This path drops back into the car park in about 300m.

> ⓘ *Lake District inhabitants used to heat their farms and cottages with peat – cut and brought down from the fells.*

▬ To shorten

For a less demanding walk without visiting the viewpoint, return to the start via the track that joins from the right just before Waypoint 2 and rejoin the main route 450m beyond Waypoint 5 (saving 45min walking time).

Ospreys

Ospreys have been nesting near Bassenthwaite Lake since 2001. A pair of birds usually returns from Africa in April and stays in the area until late in the summer, having reared up to three chicks. Watch for the white or mottled underparts of these massive, fish-eating birds of prey. The long wings are angled and have a distinctive black patch that contrasts with the white wing linings. At a distance, they could be mistaken for large gulls.

Looking into the heart of the Northern Fells

WALK 15
Skiddaw

Start/finish	Top end of Gale Road, 1.1km east of Underscar Hotel
Locate	CA12 4PH ///respected.tonality.nudge
Cafes/pubs	None on route
Transport	No public transport available
Parking	Free parking at road-end
Toilets	No public toilets on route

Time 4½hr
Distance 10km (6¼ miles)
Climb 655m

A steep, there-and-back hike to the top of England's fourth highest mountain

Skiddaw dominates many walks in this book, its looming bulk a constant presence. Attaining the 931m summit of England's fourth highest mountain might seem like a massive leap up from those routes, but walkers get a leg-up by starting at almost 300m above sea level and then following a well-constructed path almost all the way. Pick a day of good weather, give yourself plenty of time and you'll be rewarded at the top with far-reaching views and a tremendous sense of achievement.

View from the summit

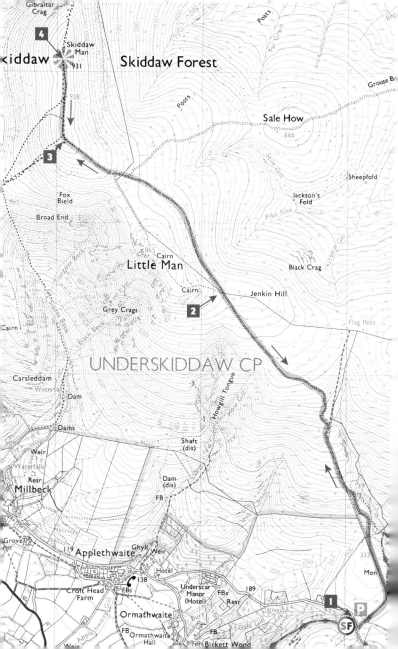

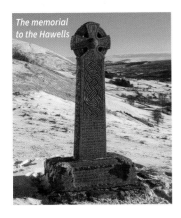

The memorial to the Hawells

stretches from Grisedale Pike in the north to Bow Fell in the south. Eventually, the gradient eases and you reach a gate on **Jenkin Hill**.

> The memorial near the bottom of Skiddaw honours the 19th-century shepherds Edward Hawell and his son Joseph, of nearby Lonscale. They were breeders of prize Herdwick sheep.

1 Go through the gate at the top of the road-end parking area and turn left – signposted Skiddaw, Bassenthwaite and Mosedale. A clear path runs beside a wall and then a fence on your left. At a fork beyond a gate, bear left, keeping faith with the fence for now and soon passing the Hawells' memorial. The climb proper begins after the next gate. Keep to the constructed path at all times. To the west, a long line of high fells

2 Go through this gate and continue on a clear path around the eastern side of one of Skiddaw's subsidiary tops, **Little Man**. The isolated range of hills to the right is known as the Northern Fells. After the next gate, a river of stones climbs to a cairn at the southern end of Skiddaw's bare and often windswept summit plateau.

3 From this cairn, swing right for the short walk north to the trig pillar, shelter and viewfinder on the summit of **Skiddaw**.

View of Derwentwater on the way up

Descending from Skiddaw, with Blencathra behind

Because of its location on the National Park's north-western edge, Skiddaw offers up an impressive outlook: to the south, there's a massed army of Lakeland fells; to the north, you're able to gaze across the waters of the Solway Firth to the Scottish hills.

4 From the summit, simply retrace your steps, remembering to keep left as you descend from Waypoint 3 and then follow the main path all the way to the base of the mountain. A right turn after the gate near the Hawells' memorial will return you to the gates leading back to the road-end parking area.

> ⓘ *The long-distance walking route, the Cumbria Way, passes through Borrowdale and skirts the base of Skiddaw on its 112km journey from Ulverston to Carlisle.*

500 million years old!

The Lake District's rocks can be divided into six main types: the Skiddaw Group, Borrowdale volcanics, Silurian slates, Coniston limestone, Carboniferous limestone and granite. The Skiddaw Group – sometimes referred to as the Skiddaw slates even though not all the rocks are slate – is the oldest. Laid down by sedimentary processes almost 500 million years ago, this group often gives rise to smooth, rounded fells such as those found in the Northern Fells.

▬ To shorten

Climb to Little Man instead of Skiddaw's main summit by taking the path on the left just before the gate at Waypoint 2. This cuts the walk by about 1hr.

USEFUL INFORMATION

Tourism organisations

Cumbria and Lake District Tourism www.visitlakedistrict.com

The Lake District National Park www.lakedistrict.gov.uk

The National Trust www.nationaltrust.org.uk

Tourist information centre

Keswick Information Centre, Moot Hall, Keswick, tel 0845 901 0845, email KeswickTIC@lakedistrict.gov.uk

Accommodation booking

Cumbria and Lake District Tourism operates www.visitlakedistrict.com/accommodation

Buses

The most useful buses for walks in this guide are:

78 from Keswick to Seatoller through Borrowdale, passing Grange and Rosthwaite

554 from Keswick to Wigton via Dodd Wood

X5 from Keswick to Workington via Dodd Wood and Braithwaite

77/77A (seasonal), circular service from Keswick, taking in Braithwaite, Whinlatter, Buttermere and Borrowdale

Boats

Keswick Launch www.keswick-launch.co.uk

Weather forecasts

Lake District Weatherline including winter ground condition reports www.lakedistrictweatherline.co.uk

Felltop forecasts www.mwis.org.uk or www.metoffice.gov.uk

In the event of an emergency

If things do go badly wrong and you or one of your walking companions needs help on the fells, first make sure you have a note of all the relevant details such as your location, the nature of the injury/problem, the number of people in the party and your mobile phone number. Only then should you dial 999 and ask for Cumbria Police, then Mountain Rescue. But remember that Mountain Rescue is a volunteer service and should be used for emergencies only. Also note that mobile reception is patchy in the Lake District, particularly in Borrowdale and in the Buttermere area.

© Vivienne Crow 2024
First edition 2024
ISBN: 978 1 78631202 0

Printed in Turkey by Pelikan Bassim using responsibly sourced paper.
A catalogue record for this book is available from the British Library.

© Crown copyright 2024 OS PU100012932
All photographs are by the author unless otherwise stated.

CICERONE

Cicerone Press, Juniper House, Murley Moss, Oxenholme Road,
Kendal, Cumbria, LA9 7RL

www.cicerone.co.uk

Updates to this Guide

While every effort is made to ensure the accuracy of guidebooks as they go to print, changes can occur during the lifetime of an edition. Any updates that we know of for this guide will be on the Cicerone website (www.cicerone. co.uk/1202/updates), so please check before planning your trip. We also advise that you check information about transport, accommodation and shops locally. We are always grateful for updates, sent by email to updates@cicerone.co.uk or by post to Cicerone, Juniper House, Murley Moss, Oxenholme Road, Kendal, LA9 7RL.

Register your book: To sign up to receive free updates, special offers and GPX files where available, register your book at www.cicerone.co.uk.